CELEBRATING

ONE HUNDRED YEARS

 of

MORRIS

BY RAY NEWELL

DESIGN BY MARK WATKINS
PRINTED BY THE LAVENHAM PRESS

Published by MMOC Ltd. © Ray Newell 2013. All rights reserved.
Printed in the UK. ISBN 978-0-9531784-0-7

CENTENARY CELEBRATIONS are rare and unique events which rightly deserve to be recognised and marked appropriately. In the case of 100 Years of Morris, much has been done to ensure that throughout 2013 enthusiasts can demonstrate and share their dedication and passion for the Morris marque. Given the worldwide success of Morris and the high regard in which surviving Morris vehicles are held, it is entirely appropriate that celebratory events are not being confined to the united Kingdom. In Europe, the United States of America, South Africa, Australia and New Zealand the Centenary is set to be recognised and celebrated at individual club and multi-make car events.

In the United Kingdom, after two years of meticulous planning, numerous events have been scheduled by individual Morris Car Clubs whose representatives continue to work tirelessly to ensure the continued use and preservation of Morris vehicles.

In addition to the scheduled Centenary events, commemorative memorabilia and collectible items have been produced. Special publications, including this one, *The A-Z of the First Morris Oxford Light Cars* produced by the Bullnose Morris Club and new books, *Morris: The Cars and the Company* by Jon Pressnell and *The New Morris Range* by David Greenslade, will add to the pool of knowledge about all things Morris.

A Heritage approved Centenary logo features on many collectible items including car badges, lapel badges, windscreen stickers, mugs and various items of clothing. One certainty for the Centenary year is that it will be celebrated with enthusiasm and style and that the celebrations will live long in the memory of those lucky enough to have participated in them.

Ray Newell

CENTENARY EVENTS 2013

28TH MARCH
100 Years of Car Making in Oxford
Mini Plant Oxford. Hosted by BMW Mini

29TH MARCH
Bullnose Morris Club Centenary Event
Nuffield Place, Nuffield, Oxon.

29TH MARCH
Morris Marina and Ital Register Centenary Event
Lakeland Motor Museum, Cumbria

18TH-19TH MAY
Beaulieu Spring Autojumble Morris Centenary Display
National Motor Museum

15TH-16TH JUNE
Morris Centenary International Rally
Cornbury Park, Charlbury, Oxon.

13TH-14TH JULY
Bullnose Morris Club Centenary Rally
Heritage Motor Centre, Gaydon

10TH-11TH AUGUST
Morris Register Centenary National Rally
Thoresby Park, Nottinghamshire

15TH-17TH NOVEMBER
Morris Centenary Centre Piece Display Stand
Indoor Classic Car Show,
National Exhibition Centre, Birmingham

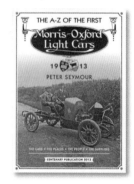

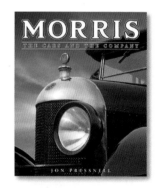

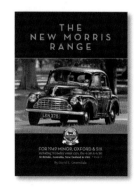

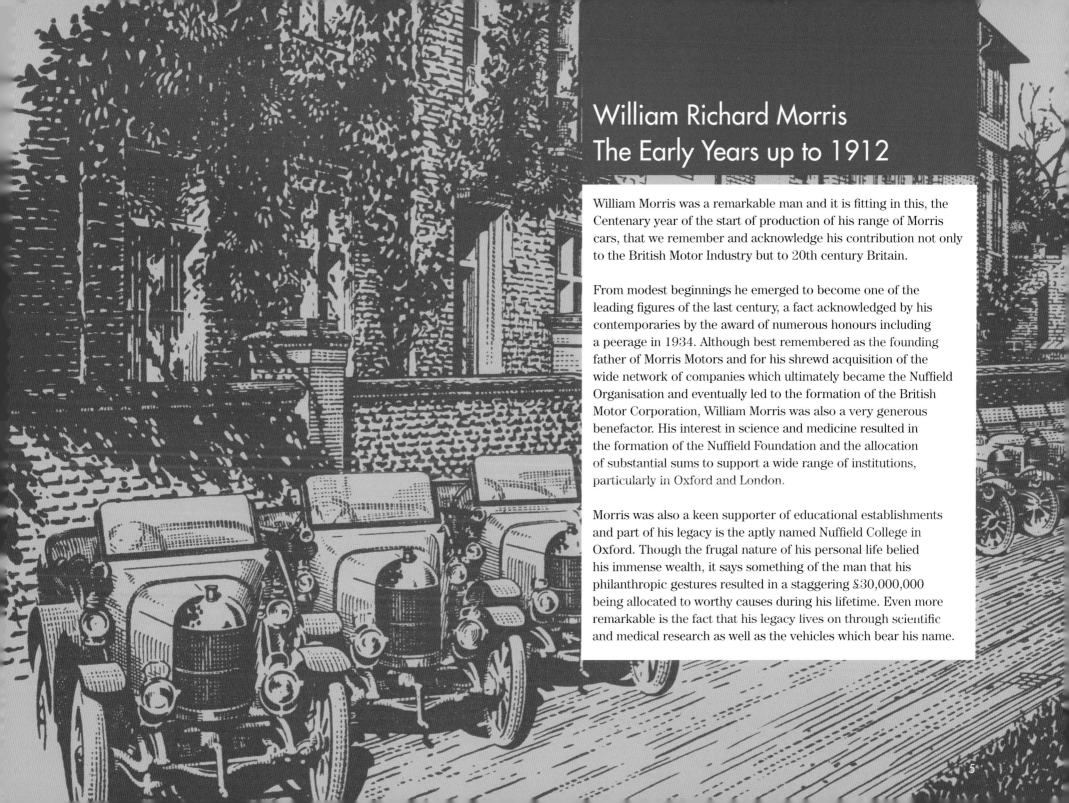

William Richard Morris
The Early Years up to 1912

William Morris was a remarkable man and it is fitting in this, the Centenary year of the start of production of his range of Morris cars, that we remember and acknowledge his contribution not only to the British Motor Industry but to 20th century Britain.

From modest beginnings he emerged to become one of the leading figures of the last century, a fact acknowledged by his contemporaries by the award of numerous honours including a peerage in 1934. Although best remembered as the founding father of Morris Motors and for his shrewd acquisition of the wide network of companies which ultimately became the Nuffield Organisation and eventually led to the formation of the British Motor Corporation, William Morris was also a very generous benefactor. His interest in science and medicine resulted in the formation of the Nuffield Foundation and the allocation of substantial sums to support a wide range of institutions, particularly in Oxford and London.

Morris was also a keen supporter of educational establishments and part of his legacy is the aptly named Nuffield College in Oxford. Though the frugal nature of his personal life belied his immense wealth, it says something of the man that his philanthropic gestures resulted in a staggering £30,000,000 being allocated to worthy causes during his lifetime. Even more remarkable is the fact that his legacy lives on through scientific and medical research as well as the vehicles which bear his name.

1891 After leaving school, aged 14, William is apprenticed to a cycle agent named Parker in Giles Street, Oxford. His remuneration is five shillings a week

1895 Morris proves his worth as an award winning cyclist becoming a racing champion at various distances while promoting his own cycle designs.

1902 Morris goes into a short-lived partnership with Joseph Cooper and successfully exhibits his first motorcycle design at the Stanley Show in London.

1877 William Morris born in Worcester on 10th October eldest son of Frederick and Emily Morris.

| 1877 | 1880 | 1891 | 1893 | 1895 | 1896 | 1902 |

1880 Morris Family leave Worcestershire and return to their native Oxford.

1896 Cycle business moves to rented property in High Street, Oxford and expands to include a repairs workshop in Queens Street, Oxford, which was later renamed Longwall Street.

1893 With capital of just £4, William Morris sets up his own cycle repair business at his parents home in James Street, Oxford.

1906 Morris begins a hire car service, operating from premises in Hollywell Road, Oxford.

1903 Morris becomes works manager of the 'Oxford Automobile and Cycle Agency', a business established by Frank Barton and Launcelot Creyke.

1907 His business interests expand to include a motor cab taxi service.

1908 William Morris sells his cycle business to concentrate on selling and maintaining automobiles.

The first Bullnose cars pictured in Hollow Way, Cowley

1911 William Morris begins to formulate his own ideas for the creation of a new British Light Car.

1903 --- 1904 --- 1906 --- 1907 -- 1908 --- 1909 --- 1911 --- 1912

1904 Morris marries Elizabeth Maud Anstey in April. However, in the same month the Oxford Automobile and Cycle Agency business failed leaving Morris in the invidious position of having to buy back his own tools at the liquidator's sale.

1909 Redevelopment of a site at Longwall Street results in the establishment of new premises called 'The Morris Garage' in 1911.

1912 WRM Motors Ltd. established on 2nd August. With financial backing to the tune of £4,000 from the 7TH Earl of Macclesfield, William Morris presses ahead with the production of his first motor car. However delays in engine production meant that he was unable to display his new creation at the 1912 London Motor Show. Armed only with blueprints for the proposed vehicle, Morris secured orders for 400 cars from Gordon Stewart of London Motor agents Stewart and Arden Ltd.

The First Cars
1913-1929

The first Morris car was appropriately named the Morris Oxford and was later designated as the 'Standard' model. In keeping with the practice successfully employed in his previous cycle business, William Morris determined at an early stage in the planning of his new motor vehicle that it would be comprised of components produced by other manufacturers.

Adopting two key principles that were to dominate his thoughts on automotive design for decades, namely producing a reliable vehicle with low running costs, Morris began his automotive business within the 'light car' sector. At the beginning of the 20th century a light car was classed as a vehicle with an engine capacity not exceeding 1500cc.

With the parameters set, Morris set about commissioning the key components for his new motor car. He was already well acquainted with the Oxford based coachbuilder Charles Raworth and Sons so it was no surprise that they were contracted to supply the bodywork. Rubery Owen, the West Midlands based company founded by the Rubery brothers in 1884, was selected to manufacture the separate chassis, while Birmingham based E.G. Wigley and Company Ltd. was the preferred choice to provide the front and rear axles as well as the steering gear. Sankey were commissioned to produce specially designed wheels.

Crucial to the success of the new car was the size, capacity and efficiency of the power unit. Morris was familiar with the work of White and Poppe with whom he had worked previously. Plans were progressed and contracts exchanged for the production of an economical four cylinder engine, a clutch mechanism and a 3 speed gearbox.

The prototype vehicle which had an open body design was assembled at the Longwall Street premises. One of the most striking features of the vehicle was the radiator design. Produced, initially by the Coventry Motor Fittings Company and then by Docherty Motor Components, its distinctive shape gave rise to the name 'Bullnose', a title which was to characterise the early cars produced by Morris.

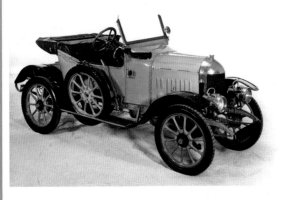

1913 William Morris exhibits his newly designed Morris Oxford light Car at the North of England Motor Show held in Manchester in February. However it was a somewhat static display given that the engine was a wooden dummy!

The following month Gordon Stewart from Stewart and Arden took delivery of the first production model and though there were some initial teething problems with the mechanical components on this particular vehicle, the initial order for four hundred vehicles was fulfilled.

Towards the end of 1913, in a separate venture, Morris successfully introduces motor buses to the streets of Oxford in order to replace the outmoded horse drawn trams. Initially this was done against the wishes of Council officials but with considerable public support.

1915 In April the new Morris Cowley was put on display for the first time. Production began in September. The bodies for this model were produced by Hollick and Pratt and amongst many American components the very modern Continental Model U engine and a very efficient 3 speed gearbox came in for much praise.

1913 — 1914 — 1915 — 1917

1914 An updated version of the Morris Oxford called the De-Luxe is announced at the 1913 London Motor Show in readiness for the 1914 season. This model featured a wider track, a longer wheelbase and a roomier interior. The size of the distinctive radiator was also increased. Morris also extended the model range to include four body styles; a two seater model, a coupe, a single seater sports version with an aluminium body and a van body with wooden panelling. During 1914, 907 vehicles were built. Morris also visited the Continental Motor Manufacturing Company in Detroit in this year to assess the viability of using American made components in his vehicles.

1914 During the First World War the companies owned by William Morris did their bit for the war effort by switching production to the manufacture of munitions. The production of bombs, grenades and mine sinkers augmented car production.

1917 William Morris is awarded the OBE in recognition of his contribution to the war effort.

1919 Morris switches engine production to the French company Hotchkiss. The engines were built in Coventry and had a capacity of 1548cc. Morris changes the name of his company from W.R.M. Motors Ltd. to Morris Motors Ltd.

1921 The British economy suffers a severe recession which adversely affects the motor industry. In the face of declining sales Morris takes the unprecedented step of reducing the cost of all his vehicles. The gamble pays off, sales increase and he ends up producing more cars than the year before.

1923 Acquisitions continue with EG Wrigley and Co Ltd. and Hotchkiss being added to the ever growing portfolio. EG Wrigley and Co Ltd. became Morris Commercial Cars while Hotchkiss was renamed 'Morris Engines Ltd'. Annual sales increase to 14,995 making Morris Britain's largest car manufacturer.

1924 A new model named the Commercial Traveller's car is introduced. Featuring a specially designed rear mounted storage compartment this model provided a useful alternative to commercial operators who did not want to purchase a van.

1919 ---- **1920** ---- **1921** ---- **1922** ---- **1923** ---- **1924** ---- **1926**

1920 A new body shop facility is built at Cowley adjacent to the old Military College in response to the growing demand for Morris vehicles.

1922 Morris begins the process of expanding his business by acquiring a number of companies who had been sub-contractors to his main business. Hollick and Pratt, suppliers of the bodies for Morris cars was renamed 'Morris Bodies' after Morris took it over. In the same year he also purchased the Osberton Radiator Company in Oxford and renamed it Morris Radiators Ltd.

1926 This was the last year that Bullnose models were produced. A replacement model dubbed the 'Flatnose', due to the introduction of a redesigned radiator, was officially announced in August 1926. The Oxford and Cowley model names continued. Morris acquires the SU Carburettor Company.

1928 The Morris Minor is launched as Morris's answer to the popular Austin Seven. Powered by an overhead camshaft, four cylinder, 847cc Wolseley derived engine and featuring fabric bodywork the cars proved popular with 12,500 being sold in the first year of production.

1927 --- 1928 --- 1929

1929 William Morris becomes a Baronet in recognition of his continuing contribution to British Industry. A new factory is built at Abingdon for the production of MG cars.

1927 The Wolseley Motor company becomes part of Morris's growing empire. In the process Morris acquires the Birmingham Ward End plant and the Adderley Park works which was later used for the production of Morris Commercial vehicles. The 1927 Oxford models have Pressed Steel bodywork, a first for a British car manufacturer.

The Bullnose Morris Club

Founded in 1952, the Bullnose Morris Club welcomes all Morris cars manufactured before December 1930.

Our focus is on keeping the cars on the road, by providing technical assistance, information and spares. Three events each year encourage the use of the cars, and the routes on these events are chosen by local Club Members. The Informal local pub meetings keep the Club Members in touch and provide essential support to those restoring or learning to maintain and drive their cars. In addition the Club also commissions a professional event organiser for tours abroad. The Club is appointed by the DVLA for expert support with regard to original Registration Marks.

The full-colour Club Magazine is published bi-monthly and contains a wide variety of technical, historical and current information on legislation and our events. A range of unique technical publications and regalia is available and complements the extensive spares service.

We have a website with a significant amount of historical information and photographs, of recent events and our Morris motor cars. The Club has strong support in Australia and New Zealand.

Membership details are available at www.bullnose.org.uk and from our Membership Secretary Malcolm McKay, Highlands, Church Lane, Little Leighs, Chelmsford CM3 1NA.

Trials, Tribulations and Triumphs 1930-1939

The British motor industry, a main stay of the British economy, was not immune to the after effects of the 1929 Wall Street crash. Morris Motors Ltd. suffered a downturn in sales, and trading profits plunged in 1931 from £1.16 million to just over £660,000. By 1933 they had reduced still further to a mere £343,000. Even drastic price cutting, including selling the Morris Minor for £100, failed to arrest the slump.

Faced with economic uncertainty and growing competition from other manufacturers including Ford at Dagenham, Morris acted decisively and appointed Leonard Lord to oversee a radical transformation of working practices at Cowley. The results were impressive. So too were the production figures which in 1935 reached an all time high. Helped by new models including the popular Morris Eight Series I, 96,500 vehicles were built. On the back of sales success, Morris Motors Ltd. emerged from the slump in a much stronger position.

Meanwhile William Morris who had acquired a new home, Nuffield Place in 1933 and been elevated with peerage to become Lord Nuffield, continued to travel widely visiting Australia and America where he sought to develop the potential for exporting and assembling Morris cars. Not all of his business ventures proved successful however. His tentative move into the Aero industry with his Wolseley Aero engines factory foundered when he failed to secure government backing.

Ironically with the onset of war he was to assume a crucial role in the Civilian Repair Organisation which was primarily engaged in the repair of damaged war planes. Part of the Cowley works was also given over to the manufacture of Tiger Moth planes which were used for training purposes for fighter pilots.

Lord Nuffield's benevolence, for which he was destined to become renowned, was already becoming noteworthy in the 1930's. His interest in medical matters led him to support local hospitals and medical research. In the wake of the harsh economic times he also set aside £2 million in 1936 to regenerate areas of Britain hardest hit by unemployment. The 'Special Areas' venture was destined to be the first of many sizeable philanthropic projects which he was to be involved in.

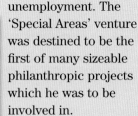

1930 In spite of continuing economic problems Morris announces the addition of the Morris Major Six to the range to add to the Morris Minor 8hp, the Morris Cowley 11.9hp, the Morris Oxford Six 15hp, the Morris Isis Six 18hp and 5cwt and 8cwt Light vans. In an effort to secure increased sales Morris markets the Morris Minor as the first £100 car.

1932 Leonard Lord joins Morris Motors and begins the rationalisation of production methods at Cowley.

1930 ---- **1931** ---- **1932** ---- **1933**

1931 William Morris adds a medical facility for employees to the ever expanding Cowley works.

1933 Morris Motors introduce the use of direction indicators to all models except the Morris Minor for 1933. A major advertising campaign is launched with approved distributors using all modern techniques including films with sound. 'Saying it with celluloid' is the catchprase of the day.

1936 The Nuffield Organisation is formed. Companies making up the Organisation include Morris Motors, the MG Car Company, Wolseley Motors, Morris Commercial Cars, Morris Industries Exports and the SU Carburettor company.

NUFFIELD N ORGANIZATION

1934 The Morris Eight Series 1 model is introduced. Destined to become the best selling Morris car of the decade this 8hp model had many attractive features including excellent performance and handling, attractive colour schemes as well as being competitively priced.

1937 The Cowley Works now employs over 5,000 people and extends to cover an area of 82 acres. The longest assembly shop under one roof is half a mile long and the longest single conveyor, believed to be the longest in Britain, measures three quarters of a mile.

1938 The Morris Ten Series M is introduced. This model was the first Morris car to feature 'monoconstruction'.

1934 ---- 1935 ---- 1936 ---- 1937 ------------ 1938 ----

1934 William Morris is awarded a peerage and selects the title Lord Nuffield.

1935 Streamlined mechanised production methods at Cowley are actively promoted to emphasis the coherent approach to vehicle production adopted there under the guidance of Leonard Lord. The term *specialisation* is coined to reflect the co-ordinated efforts of different factories producing the components required for Morris car production. Specialisation is explained as follows. *'One factory produced nothing but engines... another concerns itself solely with foundry work... a third concentrates on radiators... a fourth is devoted entirely to coachwork. The products of these four specialised factories are assembled at Cowley in the largest and best equipped motorcar assembly plant in Britain.'*

MORRIS *Specialised Production*

MORRIS MOTORS LTD
COWLEY — OXFORD

Prospective purchasers in 1938 were advised that 'the body is of all-steel construction incorporating the chassis as an integral part of the body construction'. Advantages were identified as a considerable saving in weight with increased strength and rigidity.

William Morris becomes Viscount Nuffield.

Nuffield

1938 Morris Motors Ltd. celebrate the production of the millionth Morris car. This landmark figure did not include the production figures for Morris trucks.

1939

1939 Outbreak of World War II. The switch from civilian motor car production to military hardware begins. In subsequent years, Lord Nuffield oversees the introduction of aircraft manufacture as well as the repair of other war planes.

Here Miles Thomas, Nuffield Chief Executive, and Lord Nuffield are pictured with a repaired Hurricane.

The Morris Register

The Morris Register commenced life as the 'Morris 8 Tourer Club' (M8TC). Two enthusiasts who shared a common interest in pre-war Morris 8hp tourers (Minors and Eights 1929-1939) put an announcement of the formation of the club in the motoring press in January 1960, and membership grew steadily. With the growth in membership, came the formation of regional groups, and a pattern of events, meetings and rallies that has continued until the present day.

Under pressure, the club eventually admitted Minor saloons in 1961 and Eight saloons in 1964 as associate members. Pressure to extend the scope of vehicles covered by the M8TC continued, and in 1967 a separate '10/25 Register' was established under the umbrella of the M8TC. It was also at this time that Eight saloon owners were granted full membership of the increasingly inappropriately named 'Morris Eight Tourer Club and Morris 10/25 Register', and in 1968 the name 'Morris Register' was adopted.

The club now caters for all Morris vehicles (cars, vans and commercials) designed before 1940. This includes vehicles in production from 1913 to 1953. The structure and organisation of the Register has continued to evolve, with regional groups playing a key role. Services offered by the Morris Register include an active programme of events, a monthly magazine and a comprehensive spares service.

Morris Register representatives have played an active part in the planning and preparation of the Centenary Celebrations. The Morris Register National Rally which is scheduled for the 10th and 11th August 2013 at Thoresby Hall, Nottinghamshire, will host vehicles from a variety of Morris Car and Commercial vehicle Clubs and mark another significant landmark in the history of the Club.

MORRIS TRAVELLER'S CAR 1925

MORRIS LIGHT VAN 1931

5 CWT MORRIS LIGHT VAN 1948

Morris Commercial Vehicles

Morris commercial vehicles represented a sizeable proportion of the total number of Morris vehicles produced. Car-derived light commercial vehicles proved popular and were produced in sizeable numbers, particularly in the post war years. The Morris range of heavy commercial vehicles included a wide range of large vans, lorries and special bodied vehicles which from the outset were highly regarded for their sturdy construction, mechanical reliability and versatility. Within a year of the Morris Oxford light car being introduced in 1913, a commercial variant, a light van with wooden panelling was being produced.

From 1914 onwards a modest number of these vehicles were made, however it was not until 1924 that serious consideration was given to having a separate commercial division to cater for the growing demand for heavier commercial vehicles.

MORRIS J2 VAN 1957

Morris Commercial Cars Ltd. was established in February 1924 and within two months the first large commercial vehicle, the one ton T type which was powered by a 13.9 hp Hotchkiss type sidevalve engine left the production line. By the end of 1924 some 2,487 of these models had been built. In the succeeding years other variants were introduced including a 12cwt van which also used the 13.9 hp engine. Moves to increase the weight capacity to 25cwt resulted in a new model being introduced in 1926. The Z type, as it was designated, needed more power and to meet this requirement a specially designed 15.9 hp engine was developed. This proved powerful enough for use in some larger vehicles including the 30cwt T type models.

The Versatile
MORRIS J4
DORMOBILE

Car comfort for normal everyday use-
there are seats for four.

Every week-end can be a holiday
for your family - there are beds
for two or four.

Eat when you choose-
there's a "diner" too.

Complete DORMOBILE
Caravan 2-berth Model
From £705

No Towing - No speed limit

THE DORMOBILE MOTORISED CARAVAN

ON THE MORRIS J4 VAN
Martin Walker Ltd DORMOBILE WORKS, FOLKESTONE, ENGLAND

'A Caravan in every sense of the word'

MORRIS ½ TON VAN 1959

MORRIS ½ TON PICK UP 1969

MORRIS METRO L VAN 1983

1930 was an important year for Morris commercial production as a serious move was made to enter the Heavy commercial sector. 2.5, 3, 4 and 5 ton models were built. Although production was relatively low volume at first the move into the heavy commercial sector prompted a significant change. In 1932 commercial vehicle production moved to the Birmingham based Adderley Park plant though car-derived light vans continued to be built at Cowley.

Within a year a new range of vehicles designated the C type were announced. These covered the 30cwt to five ton specification band and were powered by four and six cylinder engines. Vans, trucks and tipper lorries as well as specialist vehicles, such as ambulances and fire engines, were produced using the C type chassis. They proved popular, sold well and remained in production until 1937 when they were replaced by newly designated CV models.

Sales of Morris light commercial vehicles were dominated in the late 1920's and throughout the 1930's by 5cwt van models based on the Morris Minor and the Morris Eight. These proved popular with proprietors of small businesses as well as newly emerging fleet users. Morris vehicles proved popular with the General Post Office who ordered thousands of vans for their Telephone Engineer and Royal Mail fleets.

T2 TON 1932-38

FV 1948-53

FE SERIES III 1955-62

Other Morris models of this era included slightly larger 8cwt and 10cwt Morris vans and the Morris Series II 10cwt model introduced in 1935 which was also available as a truck with detachable wooden sides. With the outbreak of war in 1939 priorities changed across all the Morris factories as production switched from civilian vehicles to the production of military vehicles, tanks and other specialised munitions. William Morris even turned his attention to the repair of warplanes in order to assist the war effort.

In the immediate post war years the Morris Y type van, first introduced in 1940, met the needs of those requiring a 10cwt light van while the Morris Z type, 5 cwt model based on the Morris Eight, fulfilled the needs of those requiring a smaller more economical vehicle for business use. In the 15cwt/20cwt sector production resumed with the PV models. 1948 saw the introduction of diesel engines for some of the larger vans and lorries while a year later a new 10cwt van in the form of the J type entered production. It was destined to prove popular and enjoy a long production run which extended to 1957 when the original sidevalve engine was replaced by a 1489cc ohv engine and the range was redesignated the JB type.

MORRIS WE LORRY

By this time the post war Morris Minor 5cwt van and pick up models were establishing a growing reputation for economical and reliable motoring and becoming established as fleet vehicles with prestigious organisations such as the Post Office. The Morris Cowley half ton van and pick up which were marketed for a time alongside the Morris Minor variants proved popular but unlike the Morris Minor was replaced with updated Series II and Series III half ton models. By the 1960's the light commercial sector included a wide range of vans, pick ups and minibuses some of which were based on the J4 model which featured mono-construction and was available with either diesel or petrol engines. Vans and pick ups carrying the Morris badge were also available based on the famous Alec Issigonis designed Mini.

Heavy commercials of this era included a wide range of vehicles. In 1958 the popular Series III, which came in 3 and 5 ton versions using the bought-in Willenhall forward control cab, was superseded by the FF. A year later, the LC, which was a 30cwt vehicle was superseded by the FG. Later on the FG came in 2 and 5 ton versions. Characterised by their distinctive cab with hinged twin front windows they proved adaptable for a variety of uses and were widely used. The FG models which followed were more modern in design and featured a one piece screen, lower glass panels on either side of the cab and cut back cab doors.

LD VAN 1960-68

In 1962, the FH, which was visually similar to the FF, was introduced. The new model had the advantage of having the engine slanted to fit under the floor of the cab. This allowed a twin passenger seat to be fitted. In 1964 the FF was superseded by the FJ. This was designed for easier cab access, and for the first time, had a tilt cab to improve access for maintenance.

The 16/40 h.p. Morris Engine

WF 1960-1970S

However, this model suffered from mechanical difficulties in relation to cooling. The problem persisted and as a consequence the reputation of Morris as a commercial vehicle manufacturer was damaged. When the FJ range was replaced by the Laird in 1968, the Morris name ceased to be used on heavy commercial vehicles. It was replaced by the BMC badge.

In the light commercial sector however vans and pick ups continued to bear the Morris name. The ever popular Morris Minor range continued in production until 1971, with Austin variants of the Minor van and pick up being marketed alongside the more traditional Morris models. When the Morris Minor was replaced by the Morris Marina 7cwt and 10cwt van and pick up models were added to the range. These popular commercial variants were later designated as Morris 440 and 575 vans and pick ups. When Morris Ital production ceased in 1983 it fell to the Metro model to carry the Morris name for the last time. Van versions of the Austin Metro were designated as Morris 410 models though they carried the Austin Rover group logo. With their demise in 1985 the Morris name ceased to be used for production models. Optimists live in hope that at some point, the famous name may once again grace a new model. Traditionalists prefer to reflect on past glories and a rich history of commercial endeavour.

Morris Commercial Club

The Morris Commercial Club was formed in 1998 to cater for Morris commercial owners and enthusiasts as well as for ex-apprentices of Morris Commercial Cars Ltd. This collaboration has mutual benefits, in that the enthusiasts are able to obtain first hand information from some of the people who actually worked in the factory where the vehicles were built, while the former apprentices are able to revive old memories and meet up with former colleagues.

Both Morris commercial as well as similar Austin and BMC badged vehicles are eligible for club activities which include annual rallies and representation at a wide range of events held throughout the UK. Within the membership of the club there is a great deal of knowledge and expertise which is invaluable for those owning and/or restoring a Morris commercial.

The Club produces a quarterly magazine, 'Recalling', which is issued to all members. It contains historical and technical information, news from ex-apprentices' updates on discoveries and restoration projects as well as vehicles, spares and literature for sale and wanted.

The Club has a website which contains a message board, club details including membership as well as links to other clubs.

www.morriscommercialclub.co.uk

The War Years
1939-1945

The outbreak of the Second World War had a massive impact on the British Motor Manufacturing industry as a whole. At Morris Motors and other factories within the recently formed Nuffield Organisation, radical changes occurred in a relatively short space of time. A sizable number of the male work force were recruited for active service and were replaced by women who were quickly trained to take on a variety of roles within the various factories. It is estimated that the workforce throughout the Nuffield Organisation peaked at 45,000 with some 10,000 being employed during the war at Cowley. Miles Thomas who had been appointed as Vice Chairman of the Nuffield Organisation played a key role in co-ordinating the various activities which ranged from the production of Crusader tanks to the manufacture of jerry cans. Munitions, including the manufacture of torpedo shells, mines and small arms ammunition were produced in huge quantities. Vehicle manufacture was restricted to the manufacture of light reconnaissance vehicles along with special contract vehicles for military use. Some developmental work was progressed on new style amphibious vehicles and improvements on tank design.

Issigonis in 1944, testing the amphibious motorised wheelbarrow developed for the armed forces.

Lord Nuffield retained his interest in aircraft and as Director General of Maintenance RAF, he oversaw the work of the Civilian Repair Organisation which was established in 1939. During the war sizeable numbers of aircraft were repaired at the Cowley Number 1 Civilian Repair Unit and pressed back into service as part of the war effort. In total there were 1,500 repair centres in Britain. The manufacture of Tiger Moth planes, using factory style production methods was undertaken at Cowley, where other aircraft-related activities included making the wooden framework for Horsa Gliders and wing units for De Havilland aircraft.

By 1943, restrictions on the design and development of civilian motor vehicles had been lifted by the Ministry of Supply. This was welcome news to Miles Thomas who encouraged Alec Issigonis to begin the development of a new small car in readiness for the post war era. Named the Mosquito, this vehicle was destined to have a number of innovative features. However its gestation was to be beset by a number of problems, not least of which was that Lord Nuffield took an instant dislike to it. By the end of the war the Mosquito was well advanced, with a prototype model powered by a flat four engine ready for testing. Further development would prove necessary before the Mosquito would enter production as the Morris Minor.

New Models and an Export Boom 1946-1959

1948 The Morris Minor Series MM, the Morris Oxford series MO and the Morris Six MS model range is announced at the first post war London Motor Show to widespread acclaim.

In Australia, after acrimonious negotiations, work begins at Victoria Park, Sydney to build a new factory for the assembly and manufacture of Morris Cars.

1946 Civilian car production recommences with the Morris Eight Series E and Morris M Ten.

1949 American lighting regulations prompt an unexpected and unwelcome redesign of the Morris Minor Series MM frontal arrangement.

1946 --- 1947 --- 1948 --- 1949

1947 Work progresses on the Issigonis designed prototype Morris Mosquito which Lord Nuffield rather disparagingly describes as 'looking like a poached egg'. Nuffield later insists that the new small car should go into production as the Morris Minor.

The J Type Commercial is introduced to the light commercial sector. In later years it is to prove popular with the General Post Office and is used as a fleet vehicle for telephone engineers and Royal Mail deliveries.

In the years immediately following the Second World War Britain faced a tough economic situation. Rationing remained in place for several years as did restrictions on the purchase and resale of new vehicles. In an effort to secure much needed revenue the emphasis was put firmly on exporting vehicles. The Export Section which had been established at Cowley in 1933 and later renamed Nuffield Exports Ltd. was expanded in 1950 when a new CKD facility was built at Cowley. 'Export or die' was a slogan in common usage within the Nuffield organisation and by 1951 over 2,000 vehicles a week were consistently being exported to markets around the world.

In addition, in the largest markets a range of Nuffield vehicles were being assembled in specially designed plants using completely knocked down kits to which locally sourced components were added. By the mid 1950's Nuffield representatives were operating in 150 different territories throughout the world providing support for a network of dealers and distributors.

ISIS

CALLING ALL POLICE FORCES

Honours go to the greatest Morris in Morris history!

1951 Morris Motors Ltd. produces the 2,000,000 vehicle, a Morris Minor 4 door saloon which was built on Lord Nuffield's 74th birthday. In a typical benevolent gesture the vehicle is given to the Royal Institute for the Blind for fund raising purposes.

1953 One of the first tangible results of the Austin/Morris merger is the use of the 803cc ohv engine as used in the Austin A30 in Morris Minor models which are redesignated as Series II.

In May 1953 5cwt Morris Minor Series O vans and pick ups are added to the range. In October the wood framed Morris Minor Station Wagon is launched.

1955 Morris, not known for understating the virtues of their vehicles when advertising at home and abroad, excelled with their promotion of the Isis including its suitability for use by the police.

1950 --- **1951** --- **1952** --- **1953** --- **1954** --- **1955** --- **1956**

1950 In anticipation of the export boom a new facility is added at the Cowley site to cater for the despatch of CKD models. (Completely Knocked Down).

Light Commercial Morris Cowley 10cwt and Morris Oxford Traveller Series MO models introduced. Low headlamp models of the Morris Minor discontinued and four door models introduced, initially for export only.

1952 The Austin Motor Company and Morris Motors Ltd. merge to form the British Motor Corporation Ltd. In so doing they become the largest manufacturer of cars and commercial vehicles in Britain and the fourth largest in the world.

Lord Nuffield officially retires six months later.

THE BRITISH MOTOR BMC CORPORATION LTD

1954 Production of the Morris Oxford Series MO and the Morris Six MS is phased out after modest total of 12,400 Morris Six models and almost 160,000 Morris Oxfords are built.

A restyled Series II Morris Oxford replaces the Morris Oxford Series MO model while the Morris Six is superseded by the Morris Isis powered by a smooth and efficient BMC C series 2639cc engine.

1956 Alec Issigonis returns to Morris Motors Ltd. after a four year spell at Alvis and, in the wake of the Suez oil crisis, begins work on a new small car codenamed ADO 15.

The top selling Morris Minor receives a major facelift and mechanical overhaul with a reworked body shell incorporating a one piece windscreen and a very smooth 948cc engine, and remote control gearbox. It is badged as the Morris Minor 1000.

210 UXN

23

1957 A new all steel bodied, four door Morris Oxford Series IV Traveller with a 1498cc engine is announced.

1959 The Issigonis designed new small car, later to be known as the 'Mini' is launched as the Morris Mini Minor and the Austin Seven. The revolutionary design in terms of its size, transverse engine and Alex Moulton designed rubber coned independent suspension earns many plaudits when it is tested for the first time.

1957 -- 1958 ---- 1959

1958 Overseas production remains buoyant with plants in Australia, South Africa, Denmark and the Netherlands increasing the capacity for assembling BMC vehicles.

The 6/80 and MO Club

The 6/80 and MO Club was founded in 1977 following the amalgamation of two existing clubs, the Morris Oxford Club and the Wolseley Club. The Club caters for those with an interest in the Issigonis inspired Morris Oxford Series MO, the Morris Six MS, the Wolseley 4/50 and 6/80 models based on the same design as well as commercial derivatives including the J type which was based on the Morris Oxford.

The main aims of the Club are to ensure the preservation of this group of vehicles and to support owners wishing to keep these vehicles on the road. The Club boasts a truly international membership largely as a result of the large numbers of vehicles that were exported as a result of the 'export or die' initiative of the 1950's. It even has an Australasian branch which has its own committee.

Members receive an informative quarterly newsletter and have access to information regarding spares as well as a network of local groups which meet on a monthly basis. Some rare mechanical and trim parts are re-manufactured and made available to members. An active club website and members forum also provides the opportunity for a healthy exchange of ideas and opinions. The Club organises a joint annual rally and AGM, and on special occasions and anniversary events, joins with other Morris Clubs to showcase the range of vehicles the 6/80 and MO Club caters for.

Further details of the Club can be obtained from the club website www.680mo.org.uk or by contacting Pat Carroll on 01494 432797.

Mass production and Badge Engineering 1960-69

MAKING A MOTOR CAR... AS EASY AS

BMC

1961 A landmark achievement for Morris is announced on the 4th January when sales of the Morris Minor reach one million. In so doing the Morris Minor becomes the first British car to reach this milestone. To mark the occasion 349 replica Minor Million models are produced in a fetching shade of lilac and badged as Minor 1,000,000.

Morris Oxford Series VI introduced with slightly revised body styling.

1960 ---- 1961 ---- 1962

1960 Pininfarina designed Morris Oxford V saloon, powered by a B series engine continues in production having been first introduced in 1959.

1962 Morris 1100 range announced. Designed by Alec Issigonis they feature hydrolastic suspension, front wheel drive and a transverse A Series engine.

Morris Minor models are upgraded with a 1098cc engine.

After the success of the Morris Minor and the rave reviews about the new Mini Morris Minor and Austin Seven models, Alec Issigonis was heralded as an automotive genius. Unsurprisingly he continued to work under the aegis of BMC to produce progressive and innovative models to add to the already impressive range which was selling remarkably well. Next to emerge from the Issigonis drawing board was the impressive front wheel drive Morris 1100/1300 range which featured hydrolastic suspension. Destined to become the best selling British car of the 1960's, these models were marketed under the Morris, Austin, Wolseley, Riley, MG and Vanden Plas badges. The range was also extended to include Traveller models as well as a limited number of vans. Issigonis also targeted the larger car sector and was instrumental in the design of the Morris 1800 and 2200 models which were also subject to the popular practice of badge engineering.

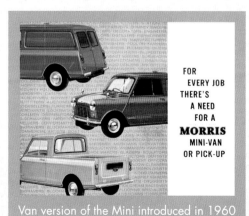

FOR EVERY JOB THERE'S A NEED FOR A **MORRIS** MINI-VAN OR PICK-UP

Van version of the Mini introduced in 1960

1963 Lord Nuffield dies at the age of 85. It is estimated that during his lifetime his philanthropic bequests totalled £30,000,000.

1965 Badge engineering, so long a feature of BMC reaches its zenith with no fewer that forty models representing Austin, Austin Healey, Morris, Wolseley, Riley, MG and Vanden Plas being actively promoted in contemporary advertising.

CHOOSE **MORRIS** THE SUCCESSFUL CARS

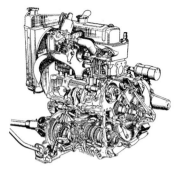

1967 An improved version of the Mini, the Morris Mini Mk II is announced. With a more powerful 998cc engine performance is enhanced still further.

1964 ---- 1965 ---- 1966 -------- 1967

1964 In the face of increasing competition from newer models in the BMC range the Morris Minor models receive a much needed revamp with improved interior trim, an amended dash board layout and revised external lighting.

1966 A Morris version of the Austin 1800 introduced in 1964 is added to the BMC portfolio. Mark II models follow two years later.

The three door 1100 Traveller is added to the 1100 range. At board room level BMC merges with Jaguar and a new company, British Motor Holdings, is created.

1968 BMC merges with Leyland to become the British Leyland motor corporation. At the time the new company is ranked as the fourth largest motor manufacturer in the world, just as BMC was when it was created in 1952.

1969 The beginning of the end for the Morris Minor is signalled with the phasing out of the Morris Minor 1000 Convertible models in June.

Sales of the Mini reach two million.

1968 - - - - - - - **1969**

Badge engineering extends to the Morris Minor range with Austin variants of the Morris Minor van and pick up introduced. Differences are confined to a changed front grille panel and Austin badges on the bonnet and steering wheel centre boss.

Alec Issigonis's contribution to the British Motor industry is recognised with the award of a knighthood.

Morris Minor Owners Club

The Morris Minor Owners Club was founded in 1976 as a result of a suggestion in the letters page of the magazine 'Thoroughbred and Classic Cars' that there should be a club for owners of the post war Morris Minor.

Enthusiastic owner, Tom Newton from Scunthorpe, took up the challenge and was immediately overwhelmed by the response. The result was a thriving club with the declared aim of seeking to ensure the continued use and preservation of the Morris Minor. Since that time thousands of owners and enthusiasts have been members of the Club. Currently membership stands at just over 11,000.

Members are provided with a range of goods, services and activities including a high quality bi-monthly magazine, Minor Matters, technical advice and guidance and access to an exclusive Club insurance scheme run in conjunction with Footman James. Cover is available for members aged between 17 and 89. The Club has an extensive network of local branches throughout the UK and has excellent links with overseas Morris Minor groups and clubs. A full programme of events is run each year and the Club is always represented at the major indoor Classic Car shows in Britain. An invaluable service which the club provides is access to rare and hard-to-find parts for early cars including Series MM and Series II vehicles.

The MMOC also has its own dedicated website and members' forum as well as a merchandising department which provides access to a wide range of clothing, books, and other car and club related items.

Details of the club and its activities are available via www.mmoc.org.uk or by telephoning the Club Headquarters on 01332 291675.

Dissention and Decline
1970-1985

1970 Morris Minor saloon production is ended in November bringing to an end twenty one years of continuous production at Cowley.

Morris Minor Traveller and commercial production moves to the Adderley Park Plant in Birmingham.

1972 The last Morris Minor built in Britain which is destined for service as a Royal Mail van leaves Adderley Park.

Marina 7cwt and 10cwt vans enter production.

1970 --- 1971 --- 1972 --- 1973

The 1970's proved to be a troubled period in the history of Morris. Under the stewardship of British Leyland Motor Corporation, industrial unrest caused massive disruption to production schedules and ultimately had a negative effect on the balance sheet. This resulted in the government taking overall control in 1974 following the publication of the Ryder Report. So far as Morris vehicles were concerned the Morris Marina took centre stage in the early years of the decade and though volume sales were confined mainly to the home market, production also took place in overseas plants where the Marina was marketed under a variety of different titles.

In Australia and New Zealand for instance the models were sold as the Leyland Marina, and in later years in New Zealand, the Marina name was dropped altogether with the vehicles marketed as Morris 1.7 and the van versions dubbed the Morris 575. In North America the imported vehicles were sold as the Austin Marina in both Canada and the United States. The Morris name continued to be used on the Marina's replacement the Ital, but when its short production run ended the Morris name ceased to be used on passenger carrying vehicles, though it was used on commercial vehicles for a little longer.

1971 The Morris Marina is introduced in April. Initially two door and four door saloons powered by 1275cc and 1800cc engines are marketed. New production methods involving overhead conveyors for transporting the Marina bodyshells to the final assembly lines are pressed into service at the Cowley works.

1973 Morris Minor production continues at the former Dominion Assembly plant in New Zealand with commercial models being the last to be assembled.

The Morris Marina range is extended by the addition of a 1.8 Estate version and sales reach 250,000. In this year it becomes the second best selling car in Britain behind its great rival the Ford Cortina.

The car that's got it all together in luxury.

1975 The 'Landcrab' Morris 1800 and 2200 models cease production after 95,271 Morris badged vehicles are built.

New Morris 18 and 22 models featuring a futuristic wedge shape design are announced along with Austin and Wolseley variants. Within a year all are re-designated and marketed as the Princess.

Slightly restyled Morris Marina Series II models introduced in October featuring a distinctive curved dash.

1980 Morris Marina production ends after one million vehicles are built, 800,000 of them for the home market. The Morris Ital takes its place. It is offered with two engine choices. Initially 1.3 A+ series (prior to use in the new Metro); 1.7 O Series

A 2.0 O Series joins in late 1980; revised front and rear styling, along with minor trim changes, distinguish it from its predecessor.

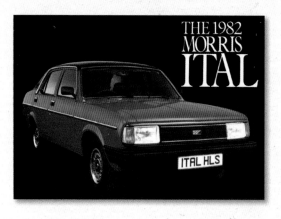

THE 1982 MORRIS ITAL

1984 Morris Ital is phased out and the Morris name ceases to be used on passenger vehicles.

1974 — **1975** — **1978** — **1980** — **1982** — **1984** — **1985**

1974 After a period of industrial unrest and increasing financial problems the British Leyland Motor Corporation is nationalised with the Government becoming the majority shareholder. The new company is simply known as British Leyland.

BRITISH LEYLAND **Morris**

1978 New O Series 1695cc overhead cam engine is fitted to the Marina Mk 3 replacing the 1.8 B series engine. Models with the new power unit are badged as 1.7.

1982 Ital production is moved from Cowley to Longbridge. 1983 upgrades include improved suspension and revisions to interior trim. Models are redesignated with former HL models marketed as SL and previous HLS as SLX.

1985 The Morris name continued in use on light commercial vehicles only, until mid 1985, the last to carry the Morris badge being the Morris 410 Metro van. The Morris name, so long a part of British motoring, is then consigned to history.

METRO

Post Production Era
1985-2013

Approximately one year after the last Morris badged passenger vehicle was produced at Longbridge, the Ital presses and supporting plant for producing the bodyshells was moved to China, where it was modified to produce four variants of a vehicle which was officially designated as the Huandu model 9105. Essentially these were estate and van versions of the Morris Ital with the exception of being powered by different engines and fitted with alternative suspension parts. Production of the Huandu in China lasted until 1999.

Apart from this Chinese venture and the continued production of Hindustan models in India, links to the Morris heritage in terms of motor manufacturing are tenous at best. It has fallen to former employees, enthusiastic owners and fans of the Morris marque as well as those tasked with preserving examples of Morris vehicles in museums, particularly in the newly created Heritage Motor Centre in Gaydon Warwickshire, to perpetuate the Morris name and ensure that the history of Morris is documented for the benefit of future generations of owners and enthusiasts.

The establishment of Clubs dedicated to the use and preservation of the Morris marque, as well as derivatives of the considerable range of vehicles produced, has done much to raise the level of interest amongst the public at large. Given the success of the export drive particularly in the 1950's and 1960's this has not been confined to Britain. In countries worldwide clubs exist for the purpose of bringing together like minded enthusiasts who wish to use, maintain, restore and preserve their Morris vehicles. In turn this has led to the establishment of a thriving business community dedicated to the re-manufacture of parts and the sourcing of new old stock components.

THE MORRIS MOTORS BAND

One of the more unusual aspects of the post production era was the effort made to continue the tradition of the Morris Motors Band. The band was originally formed in 1924 and consisted of employees based at the Cowley works in Oxford. In the notes that accompanied their numerous recorded albums, reference was frequently made to the fact that many of the band members were equally as skilled in the playing of their instruments as they were as craftsmen in the factory. The band, under the musical direction of Harry Mortimer, justifiably earned an international reputation for excellence and apart from touring in Holland, Switzerland and Scandinavia performed regularly on BBC radio.

To transport the band members and their equipment two different coaches were built during the time the band was in existence. One has been restored and resides at the Oxford Bus Museum. It is scheduled to attend some of the Centenary events scheduled for 2013 and will be in attendance at the International Rally at Cornbury Park.

Although the Morris Motors Band has ceased to exist their music lives on in the many recordings which were made. Now collectors' items, these can still be found in both LP and tape recorded formats. No doubt the music may form part of the celebrations of 100 years of Morris during 2013.

PRE-WAR MINOR NETWORK

The PWMN was established in May 2008 as an internet resource for enthusiasts of the pre-war Morris Minor. The website today is home to some 2700 images, 650 period articles, and much more beside. Amongst the period items are road test reports, vehicle maintenance and technical papers, original brochure images and specifications as well as general feature articles. The website's pages and Discussion Forum are regularly visited by the Network's 450 + members from over 50 countries worldwide.

In early 2009 further pages were created for enthusiasts of the 1929-1932 M.G. 8/33 Midget or 'M' Type and the 1930-31 Wolseley Hornet, both models being very close relatives of the Morris Minor. For the future, the Network will strive to grow its internet resource base by continuing to add relevant material to the site, while also organising regular events at which fellow enthusiasts can meet and use their cars.

www.prewarminor.com

THE MINOR LCV REGISTER

The Minor LCV Register is dedicated solely to the preservation, use, restoration and historical study of all Minor LCVs (both Austin & Morris) in any condition and wherever they are! In keeping with the essence of the Register's conviction, vehicles from the dilapidated to the delightful are catered for from around the world.

For full details contact
Brian Lee (Minor LCV Register)
Laurels
45 Frederick Rd, Warley,
West Midlands. B68 0NX
Phone 0121 422 1334

Email: RussLCV@gmail.com
www.MinorLCVreg.co.uk

POST OFFICE VEHICLE CLUB

The Post Office Vehicle club was formed in 1962 by a group of people whose interest in the General Post Office fleet started during the inter-war period. Since then the Club has evolved, to the extent that it now covers both past and current vehicles owned and operated by the GPO, The Post Office and BT.

The principal aims of the Club are to bring together like minded people who have an interest in the vehicles used by the Post Office and the historical records which are maintained by the club. These cover the period 1906 to the present day.

The Club produces a monthly magazine 'Post Horn' which keeps members informed about current vehicles in use with the Royal Mail, Parcel Force and BT fleets. It also provides information for owners of 'Preserved Vehicles' and publishes concise guides which contain information about vehicles purchased from 1906 to the present day.

For anyone owning or aspiring to own a Post Office or General Post Office vehicle and who requires information about the history of the vehicles used in the past then this is the club for you.

www.povehclub.org.uk

THE J, J/B AND 101 REGISTER

The J, J/B and 101 Register caters for owners and enthusiasts of just one vehicle – the Morris Commercial J-type, and its later variants, the Morris J/B and the Austin 101. 2013 is the 65th Anniversary of the J-type, which was announced at the 1948 Commercial Motor Show at Earl's Court. Production started in 1949 with the last vans being registered in 1961.

We have an award-winning website at www.jtypevan.com which is continually being added to.

Historical research is ongoing, whilst we also help members find spares for their vans and answer postal and telephone enquiries regarding membership, insurance valuations, details required for the retention of original registrations or acquisition of age-related number plates, plus the many enquiries that we have from owners needing help in proving the age of their vehicle – in order that the benefit of Road Tax-exemption is gained.

MORRIS MARINA OWNERS CLUB AND ITAL REGISTER

Frank Phillips and Clive Higgins founded the Morris Marina Owners Club, incorporating the Ital Register in 1985, with the intention of recognising the place of the Marina and Ital in British motoring history. The club currently has well over 300 members across the world, all of whom have access to an informative club publication 'Understeer', advice on technical matters as well as access to an informative web based forum.

The Marina & Ital were the last solely Morris badged passenger cars to be sold after a long and illustrious marque history and the members of the Club committee seek to promote the vehicles in a positive and constructive way with the aim of preserving as many surviving Marina and Ital vehicles as possible. Whether you wish to be an active member, want to join for access to spares or just for the reassurance that help is at the end of a phone then a warm welcome awaits. By joining the Club you can help to ensure the survival of these popular and successful Morris Cars.

For further information contact Chris Weedon on 01234 407518 or visit www.morrismarina.org.uk

MORRIS COWLEY & OXFORD OWNERS CLUB

The club was set up originally to encourage and assist with the preservation of Morris Oxford, Morris Cowley and Morris Isis models produced from 1954-1960. The following models are catered for. Cowley 1200 and 1500, Oxford Series II, III and IV, Isis Series I and II as well as Half ton commercial variants. More recently the club has expanded the model range to include the Indian produced Hindustan Ambassador.

Though a small club, the enthusiastic and hard working committee seeks to provide owners of these fine motor cars with an informative magazine three or four times a year, offer technical advice, source parts and information in order to keep surviving models in active use and provide support to owners seeking to restore surviving models.

Club contact details:
Treasurer/Magazine Editor
Derek Andrews 01225 766800
jones@jpamela.orangehome.co.uk

Oxford & Cowley spares/
technical advice
Richard Monk 01342 841625
richkaty1@ntlworld.com

Isis spares/technical advice
Howard Dent 01865 739157
howard@racingphoenix.com

CAMBRIDGE-OXFORD OWNERS CLUB

The Cambridge-Oxford Owners Club is the largest club catering for all BMC 4 and 6 cylinder Farinas and pre Farina Austin vehicles. Founded in 1980 the Club offers members access to a Quarterly Club magazine, the opportunity to attend local, regional and national events as well as a range of technical advice and information. An informative website includes a buyer's guide and an owner's guide.
Club contact: Taff Gillingham
taff@taffmail.demon.co.uk
www.co-oc.org

LANDCRAB OWNERS CLUB INTERNATIONAL

The Landcrab Owners Club International (LOCI) was established to cater for the needs of owners of Morris and Austin 1800/2200 and Wolseley 18/85 and Six models produced between 1964 and 1975. These models are more popularly known as Landcrabs. The Club's main aim is to increase the profile of these vehicles in by organising club rallies and events, showcasing the cars at major British Classic car shows, sourcing and arranging for the manufacture of new components and acting as a focus for Landcrab enthusiasts worldwide through the quarterly Club publication 'Landcrab News'.
Club contact: Clive Serrell
01527 65824
www.landcrab.net

THE BRITISH MINI CLUB

The British Mini Club was established in 1992 offering membership to thousands of Mini owners and enthusiasts worldwide. The club caters for all Minis including the Morris Mini Minor models dating back to 1959. One of the highlights of the year is British Mini Day which always attracts a huge entry featuring both Classic and Modern Minis.
Club contact: David Hollis
01384 897779
www.britishminiclub.co.uk

THE 1100 CLUB

The 1100 Club was formed in 1985 to cater for owners of the BMC 1100/1300 range of cars including Morris, Austin, Wolseley, MG, Riley and Vanden Plas. The aim of the club is to provide members with technical help, support and information and to keep as many 1100/1300 cars on the road for as long as possible. The Club produces an informative bi-monthly magazine called 'Idle Chatter'. The Club also owns and maintains a 'Skeleton Austin 1100' which was displayed at the Geneva Motor Show. It can be viewed at the Stondon Motor Museum, near Henlow, Bedfordshire
Club contact: Chris Bryant
chairman@the1100club.com
www.the1100club.com

2013 and Beyond

The Centenary of Morris has already been marked in a significant way by various Clubs and organisations during 2013 in the UK and elsewhere in the world.

As a result of the co-operation between various Morris Clubs based in the UK in planning a co-ordinated programme of events for 2013, it is hoped that a legacy of the Centenary Celebrations will be the establishment of an Association of Morris Car Clubs.

A concensus already exists that this idea should be progressed so that in a spirit of mutual co-operation the links which have been established over the past three years can be maintained.

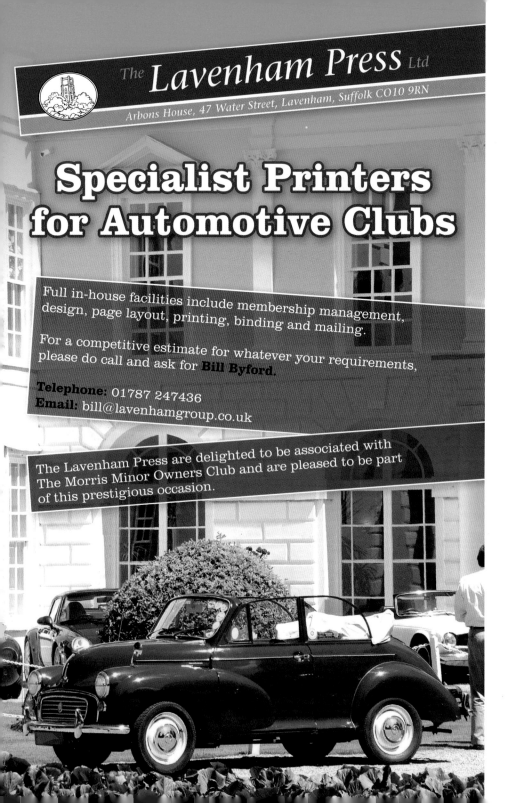

The Lavenham Press Ltd

Arbons House, 47 Water Street, Lavenham, Suffolk CO10 9RN

Specialist Printers for Automotive Clubs

Full in-house facilities include membership management, design, page layout, printing, binding and mailing.

For a competitive estimate for whatever your requirements, please do call and ask for **Bill Byford.**

Telephone: 01787 247436
Email: bill@lavenhamgroup.co.uk

The Lavenham Press are delighted to be associated with The Morris Minor Owners Club and are pleased to be part of this prestigious occasion.

ACKNOWLEDGEMENTS

I am indebted to many people who through their help have made it possible for this centenary publication to be produced. First and foremost I wish to thank the members of the National Committee of the Morris Minor Owners Club for their support and encouragement to produce a publication worthy of celebrating the Centenary of Morris and for agreeing to publish it in conjunction with Lavenham Press. Bill Byford and Terence Dalton have also been unstinting in terms of their practical support in arranging the printing of this commemorative publication.

Grateful thanks are also due to the British Motor Industry Heritage Trust, to the Press Office at Mini Plant Oxford and the Oxford Bus Museum for access to historical images and permission to reproduce them. Without the assistance of various Club representatives it would not have been possible to include such a wide range of illustrations and I am particularly indebted to Rob Symonds of the Morris Register for his assistance in sourcing factual information and allowing me access to his collection of published materials and photographs. In this regard, Nicola Parkins has also been generous in allowing the publication of her photographs taken at the Centenary event at Nuffield Place in March 2013. In a true spirit of collaboration contributions in the form of access to brochures, photographs of club events, club logos, historical images and advice have been received from the following people: Sandy and Rosie Hamilton, Margaret and Monty Goding, Nigel Harrison, Clive Brown, Gerald Newbrook, Pat Carroll, Howard Dent, Chris Lambert, Trevor Ford, Brian Ford, Harvey Pitcher, Alan Scott, John Colley, Russell Harvey and Keith Fletcher.

Mark Watkins of Luck Design has worked tirelessly to ensure that the original concept for this publication has been adhered to. Without his contribution it would have been impossible to do justice to the achievements of Morris within the parameters set. To anyone else who has contributed in anyway and who I may have inadvertently omitted to mention may I belatedly add my thanks.

Ray Newell